taurus

april 21

may 20

WHITE STAR PUBLISHERS

contents

Text by
Patrizia Troni

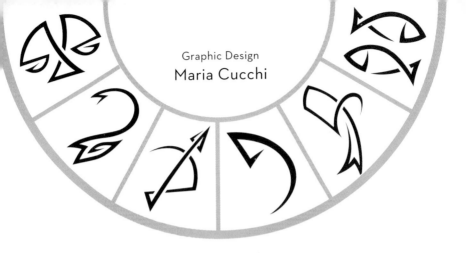

Graphic Design
Maria Cucchi

Character and Temperament

After the incandescent, explosive energy of the first sign in the Zodiac, Aries, everything acquires quite another rhythm with Taurus. Life is no longer something that burns out in an instant with all its might, but something whose intensity is to be guided, modulated, kept under control, and led in the direction of advantageous utility and absolute concreteness. Therefore, your temperament is that of a basically peaceful and tranquil – but by no means passive or inert – character. Taurus represents serene power that is in sync with the natural world like no other sign, expressing vitality that is continuous and often powerful, with a sensuality that is, at the same time, equilibrium, harmony, and control over the vortex of energy that never diverges from the force of nature.

Everything in this harmonious universe occupies a primary position, everything has its very own place, and this 'territoriality' regards your character, which tends, more or less consciously, to preserve, enhance, expand and make fruitful its own environment. The natural world, in which everything is harmonious equilibrium, also requires continuous attention, which means care, continuous work, stamina, and the capacity to create a warm and reassuring sphere of affection. Consequently,

Taurus is a hard, tireless worker with a great deal of physical resistance, concrete and realistic: you love facts more than empty dreams and senseless fantasies.

Taurus conquers happiness through constancy and organization, with a utilitarian awareness of the value of things and how to conserve them, without however slipping into neurotic tension and without losing contact with that natural spirit that never loses sight of the physicality and well-being of the body.

Their character is fundamentally lacking in aggression and imbalance, and their rare fits of anger occur when the abode of peace that their 'I' has built around themselves is challenged or threatened due to some difficulty or other. But, they always seek stability, which is achieved through daily commitment and with a slow, progressive rhythm, which methodically increases their performance and possessions. True, this might sometimes lead them to a certain degree of materialistic possessiveness and greed, but this is because they have made a great effort, and it has cost them a lot, to attain what they own.

Their determination and will power do not appreciate being challenged by enigmas, confusion and uncertainty. Although they know how to use their brain when necessary, they never use it too much, and their reasoning is always connected to a practical approach that slowly but surely leads to positive results.

Taurus is like fertile, luxuriant earth, like a large, solid and indestructible oak tree that those who love them lean upon. They are discriminating, excellent administrators capable of a relaxed and easy-going vision of life, examples of well-being and fine management. They do not like unnecessary risks, provocation, and wasted effort; with their slow pace and well-focused approach they proceed to create a good life for themselves. They act with sobriety and calm that sometimes becomes imperturbable, and with great energy that, however, is also placid and never veers from its well-balanced approach. Taurus avoids distress and complications; they cannot tolerate the insane competitiveness that makes one insensitive and anxiety-ridden. They are prudent and dislike society events and silly distractions. People may sometimes accuse them of being monotonous, but will eventually realize that they are a steadfast, reliable point of reference that they need and can depend upon.

Love and Passion

Taurus is ruled by Venus and the Venusian nature is revealed in the great importance they attach to love and sensuality. Love for them is a basic hub around which their whole life revolves and develops. Although their extraordinary sensuality is always receptive to the powerful attraction of the flesh, and though sexuality is, in their opinion, one of greatest pleasures in existence, in matters of love they are constructive. They want to achieve a relationship that does not generate chaotic emotions or confused transgression, but rather harmony and accord that grows stronger day by day, becoming the heart of a domestic context that, over the years, creates an intimate world of great warmth and stability.

Love is not cerebral, contorted, perverse or troubled. No, for Taurus love is pleasure and beauty, sweet abandon and the greatest physical intensity. Love is something that they feel is theirs in every part of their body and that becomes visceral. Their love is precisely 'theirs', which sometimes leads to the occasional attack of jealousy or possessiveness, and no buts about it. The person at their side must be loved with total, protective, almost maternal attention. The relationship must nev-

er proceed by means of conflict, arguments, strange games, guile and subterfuge. Everything in love must be clear and solar, and agreement is immediately an accord of the flesh and physical vibrations that is expressed in spontaneous and natural eroticism. Their desire is also the powerful and pacific desire of a grand nature that they consider an expression of concrete, material harmony. Therefore, their feelings are never the mawkish, cloying expressions of a false and irritating sweetness. Their tenderness lends strength and energy to their partner, a sensation of support that transmits strength, slowly and powerfully amplifying the voice of a passion that is fiery but not blind and unbalanced.

Therefore, the common path toward the most intense pleasure is a sweet and solid progression that does not want to squander everything in a few minutes, but enjoy lovemaking moment after moment, slowly, with total, absolute intensity. There is no separation between the heart, mind and body in your loving. Loving someone means desiring, and desiring means seeing to their partner's every need, immediately.

They transmit their highly developed practical sense into a dynamic of love as well, but planning cannot, by any means be the essence of a relationship. For them, love must be true love, which means that 'constructive policy' and desire are one, never separate. At times this may create some contradictions, because in the long run love based solely on physical attraction does not suffice for Taurus, yet the life of a couple experienced only as the concrete sense of material construction makes no sense to them if physical attraction is lacking. Falling in love starts off from reciprocal physical pleasure, from a vibration that tenderly touches all the fibers of their being, but this sensual magnetism must be followed by a continuity that becomes common participation in a real and grand project. Thus, it is not mere adventure – however exciting that may be – that attracts them, nor is it seduction. Love is a central pillar that is too important to be transformed into a sterile game of conquests.

They are more than willing to listen to their partner and often behave wisely and patiently with him or her. Those who love them sink into their large, sweet eyes, which impart all the regenerative and revitalizing power of natural harmony.

How to Hook a Taurus and How to Let Them Go

If you want to seduce a Taurus, you must start from a key concept. Taurus is a sign strongly connected to the five senses of sight, hearing, taste, smell and touch. In order to win their heart it is important to tantalize and satisfy their senses. Taurus likes to see their partners smiling, harmonious, sensual, and natural, without any artifice or affectation. They like to hear a voice that is sweetly firm, calm, relaxed, and persuasive. They like to smell, touch, and perceive the chemistry that erupts when two bodies meet and touch. They also like to 'taste': when Taurus loves and desires they taste the other person as if they were pastries.

In order to seduce a female Taurus the secret is to invite her to dinner in a first-class restaurant, preferably in a natural setting with a spectacular view and intimate atmosphere. Again, take long walks with her by the river, in a forest, or propose an excursion in the mountains or a picnic in the countryside. You must be reassuring and measured, yet steadfast. It is best to look her straight in the eye and show her how much you love children and large families. In order to seduce a male Taurus one good idea is to invite him to your home for dinner, welcoming him with the scent of a pie just taken out of the oven and offering him dishes not necessarily elaborate, but tasty. You need not be a chef; what is important is that he understand your love of food and good cooking. He will appreciate, and be won over by, the fact that you shop for local produce, are very judicious in your choice and pay attention to the prices. In order to break your relationship with a Taurus, however, you must bear in mind that this will be like stabbing them in the chest. For Taurus, accepting a separation is a painful and laborious process. A slow withdrawal, progressive coolness and absence, are much better than a sudden break. However, should you want to end the relationship rapidly, it is best to betray them openly, because they will almost certainly be unable to accept this and forgive you.

Compatibility with Other Signs

Taurus is in splendid harmony with Cancer and Pisces. With the former, Cancer, a circle of warmth and tenderness is generated magically, a circle that protects them from the uncertainty and confusion of the world, with extremely intense eroticism. In the case of the latter, Pisces, their realistic and pragmatic nature allows itself to be transported into incredible worlds of dreams and lively imagination, at times attaining heights of passionate romanticism that they would never want to end. With Scorpios, there are often explosions of great erotic intensity, but they entail suffering due to abandonment on the part of one of the two signs and oscillating phases of exaggerated possessiveness. Taurus is quite compatible with Virgo and Capricorn, with whom they can establish long-lasting and deep relationships, although there is the risk of their becoming somewhat monotonous. The Aries character is, perhaps, too peremptory and dominating for their taste, just as Leo's egocentricity is not always gratified by their essential style, which is little inclined to extol a personality so much in need of approval. Among the Fire signs, a relationship with a Sagittarius is better, since Taurus appreciates their direct, frank and passionate approach. Taurus likes Geminis, and they lend a good deal of carefree lightness to their character. Although many relationships are established between Taurus and Libra, the doubt and hesitation typical of this Air sign might make you feel the need for a stronger, and more determined partner. With Aquarius, there is the risk of extremely pleasant 'fatal attractions'. However, their elusive and overly self-sufficient, unrestrained character clashes with Taurus' need for a secure and constant relationship. Finally, Taurus matches well with Taurus, but this may be more a question of a professional, working relationship rather than the development of a truly open, surprising and rewarding love story.

Taurus Profession and Career

For a practical, concrete personality like Taurus, work always takes priority over any other matter. Only hard work allows them to attain that condition without anxiety and anguish that guarantees serenity in their existence. In work they are scrupulous, capable of organizing their various tasks quite efficiently; they can be humble and, at the same time, remarkably determined. While their colleagues raise the white flag and give up trying, they are still there resisting, and manage to get to the bottom of the matter. They are never hasty, feverish or superficial at their workplace. In everything they do, they have recourse to patient effort and conscientious and constant concentration. Their strong will and tenacity are truly remarkable, and their physical stamina, calm and patience are important gifts that they use to the best advantage.

With their serious, reliable professional approach they achieve important positions in their career. This does not mean that they habitually seek support or connections in high places. Nothing arrives like manna from heaven; Taurus is not the type of person who opens the trapdoor and finds a treasure that allows them to live in luxury without working. On the contrary, they deserve everything they earn. Their success is due to steady concentration, tranquil commitment that does not admit of useless distraction and tenacity that can become downright stubbornness, as well as their good-hearted nature, which creates a harmonious atmosphere in their workplace.

Their proverbial frugality has led some to accuse them of being misers. But, more than avarice, this should be called wisdom, the awareness that periods of abundance can easily give way to serious straits and that the unexpected is always lying in wait just around the corner. Therefore, they are quite adept at setting aside the fruits of their labor and investing it brilliantly. While managing money, they are never carefree, silly speculators who risk everything with the mirage of improbable big earnings. No, they build their wealth gradually, paying constant attention to the performance curve, which must always indicate a slow but evident increase. If it doesn't, then they become anxious.

Whatever profession Taurus is engaged in, be it as an entrepreneur or employee, their reliability and the excellence, both quantitative and qualitative, of their dedication to their work are qualities that are always evident. As managers or entrepreneurs, they always act prudent-

ly and with careful, methodical thought, without exposing themselves recklessly and without being misled or blinded by twists or novelties that have not been carefully assessed beforehand. As employees, they always earn the total trust of their superiors both for the precision of their work and for the amount of work they manage to attend to. They are excellent collaborators because they distinguish themselves for your discreetness, honesty, precision and concreteness. You always put your words into action.

It is a well-known fact that everything connected with food and eating is connected to Taurus. Consequently, they make fine foodstuffs dealers, cooks, producers of agricultural products, wines and liquor, as well as industrialists or employees in firms that produce pots, pans, plates, kitchen sets and the like. Many people born under Taurus also have a flair for holistic and natural medicine, including dieticians and chiropractors, and even psychologists or psychoanalysts in some cases (we must not forget that Freud was Taurus). But, whatever profession you practice, usually your career will consist of a constant rise and improvement, until you reach the heights of excellence in your field.

How Taurus Thinks and Reasons

One must not mistake your gift of reflection and pure intelligence for cunning, astuteness and a propensity for rapid deception. Taurus intelligence is slow but inexorable, from a logical standpoint. Precisely because you always adhere to concrete data and actual facts, at times your method of reasoning may lack those intuitive and illuminating flashes of those who grasp everything at once. Taurus ponders, places all the data at their disposal on the table and evaluates them one by one, slowly, without being seized with apprehension. Even though they spend more time than others in calculating that two plus two makes four, when you arrive at four there's no stopping you. The truth they have learned becomes absolute, indisputable, and unconditional. It is no accident that many great philosophers were Taurus, including Kant and Wittgenstein, and the latter's famous statement, "What we cannot speak about we must pass over in silence" suits Taurus to a T. Also true is that Taurus lacks a some imagination and can't claim to be experts in intuitive logical connection. Their manner of reasoning is based on evidence and always results in their finding a truth that may be simple and direct but is, in any case, absolute. They also have a remarkable gift for listening to people, which limits itself to what is heard without too much expectation – another indication of their excellent capacity to see things for what they really are. They attach importance to that which really exists, what they can see, what is tangible and evident. They want to see things with their own eyes, touch them, before reaching any conclusion.

If people sometimes accuse them of being scarcely perceptive, of not always having their antennae in sync with their surroundings, they can reply that it may be true that they see little, but what they do see is quite clear.

It is a rare thing indeed for Taurus to be bewildered, confused, or led astray by incongruous feelings and agitation. It is also rare to see Taurus backpedal. When they have come to a conclusion, have formed an opinion, made a decision or expressed an idea, it is difficult, if not downright impossible, to dissuade them from taking that course.

Sometimes the defect in their mode of reasoning may lie in their slow pace and intuition is not exactly their forte. The tempo of elaboration of their thoughts is connected to their astrological DNA, which is that of a ruminant and their thoughts revolve around themselves until a solution is found. But, in the end, thanks to their realism and concrete nature they hardly ever make a mistake in evaluation.

Taurus is not cerebral and does not like the pure abstraction of those whose thinking process becomes continuous torment. In their opinion, the mind is never disconnected from the physicality of the body. They reason well when their body feels relaxed and immersed in harmonious well-being, when their body feels well and no one pressures them or makes them nervous. They do not like obscure labyrinths, nor are they fond of exhausting themselves in continuous gloomy meditation. For Taurus, intelligence is a useful instrument that must improve the quality of life, not a display of intelligence as an end in itself. While they do not disdain levelheaded dialog and dialectics, they dislike getting hopelessly involved in interminable, maddening and sterile discussions. The conclusion reached must be corresponded by its immediate practical application. Thinking is useful in improving action and obtaining the best results in life. They are not pseudo intellectuals who play and enjoy themselves with their neurons, making a grand display of pure intelligence. They want essential, simple truth. Their truth.

Sociability, Communicatior

and Friendship

If we define sociability as the continuous, endless kaleidoscope of nightlife, in which 'happy hours', events and parties of all kinds alternate, then the level of sociability of Taurus would be considered quite low indeed. In general, they tend to keep their distance from noise and confusion that only dull the mind and, above all, destroy the intimate and authentic atmosphere they prefer. But, if sociability means being attentive to others, listening closely and relating to them, the sheer pleasure of creating accord with their questioner that develops in a slow, relaxed manner, then their level of sociability is most certainly very high.

Taurus is connected to everything related to the clan, the family, and, in most cases, the relationships that please them most are those established with those who, over the years, have created profound harmony with them and a bond that is often familial, that is, a family-like tie. Their ideals are a large, numerous family that, with time, grows with the arrival of new children; a house, preferably in the country; and vivaciousness which expresses a lifestyle that is dynamic but is an integral part of an atmosphere of profound affection. In the abstract, they do not like strangers. At the beginning of every acquaintanceship there is a bit of mistrust on their part. They open their heart slowly and, often the process of becoming acquainted or friends takes months and months before they feel it is an authentic relationship. Although in your work, or for practical reasons, you find no difficulty in communicating with others, and on the contrary, for the most part prove to be brilliant and sympathetic, the steady flow of acquaintanceships required in everyday life is by no means the objective of their life. By nature, they are somewhat taciturn, even closed and unreceptive at times. Their placid nature, which needs peace and harmony, strongly dislikes long discussions, frequent handshakes, and even exhausting argumentation. If there is something that must be said or clarified, they prefer to do it right away without roundabout phrases, and, at times, some of their peremptory statements could seem a bit coarse and brusque. However, they strongly dislike arguing, they are not provocative people who throw down the gauntlet on every occasion. In their opinion, the best conversation is the one that takes place among a very limited number of people, perhaps while sipping a glass of wine or during an intimate dinner. It is here that their surprisingly ironic and light-hearted side might come to the fore. If someone should argue insistently, oppose their stance, try to convince them of an idea at all costs, or speak and act in an arrogant and aggressive manner – which is the worst possible scenario – then they might very well lose their proverbial patience which might be a portent that trouble is brewing. When a Bull is forced into the arena, he might lose all his self-control – although, in truth, this happens very rarely.

Taurus is rather selective in friendship. They're not the type with a thousand friends, friends everywhere they go. A few friends, but trustworthy, faithful ones – this is the line most frequently adopted by Taurus. While in normal, everyday life they do not squander money or waste resources, in the case of a special friendship they can be very generous should their friends really need something. And, they are certainly not nagging, irritating or intrusive friends. Where friendship is concerned, they have a healthy sense of moderation and respect that, in the long run, generates a feeling of assurance, well-being and true affection in the other person.

When Taurus Gets Angry

Basically, Taurus is tranquil and mild. You have an almost infinite spirit of tolerance and your phlegm is admirable. If people leave you in peace in your pasture and if no one invades your territory or threatens your clan there is very little chance of conflict. But, should you be forced into the bullring and a host of banderillas is thrown at you, it will not be easy for those who attacked you to escape unscathed. Just as Taurus, the bull, lowers its head and charges at the matador once it is in the arena, when they are angered they move with all the power of their strong, resistant and stubborn spirit. And, it will not be easy to placate them. It is best not to annoy them, because their rage is unexpectedly violent. And prolonged.

Material safety is very important for Taurus. Their partner must be careful not to indulge in extravagant shopping sprees, use their credit card in a carefree manner or spend a lot of money before having spoken to them about it. Wasting or squandering money makes them lose their temper. Those who have a relationship with a Taurus, be it based on business or friendship, must be careful not to get on their nerves, not to pressure them or force them into an unpleasant situation. Most of all they must not trigger suspicion in Taurus, because if something seems to be wrong they may well mull over it, and then the time will come to settle accounts. The Taurus character is not very conciliatory. They demand facts and explanations, and, if they do not receive them, they are quite capable of breaking off all relations. And, once they sever a relationship of any kind it is very unlikely that it will ever be resumed. Taurus is extremely possessive; what is theirs is theirs. In order not to anger them, others should not meddle in their affairs or take what belongs to them. When they lend something - and by so doing they show that they have the greatest trust in the other person - it should be returned as soon as possible.

Taurus
Children

Children born under the sign of Taurus are like a young plant, a shoot that, little by little, strikes deep roots in life. And, their roots are nourished by everything that is beautiful, harmonious, colorful, and invigorating for both the body and spirit. Their soul absorbs and takes in everything. From a very early age, they show interest in everything around them, practical things, the behavior and acts of those close to them. It is very important that Taurus children not be left alone for any length of time. They must feel protected and not neglected. They need to be surrounded by the affection and attention of their family, sentiments that they will repay with interest when they themselves become adults. Their life is based on the family - grandparents, uncles and aunts, and cousins - like a warm nest, a reassuring embrace that must never be lacking.

Taurus children like to shop on their own, and it would not be a bad idea to give them a small allowance from the time they are still very young, because they have an innate sense of saving and frugality, and the little bit of money that will increase in their piggy bank will not only make them responsible, but will also give them a pleasant sense of security. From an early age, they manifest good taste, do not like to appear unkempt, and tend to be choosy about their clothes. Prone to sulking, being bad-tempered and resentful because of their innate obstinacy, but also extremely sensitive, Taurus children can be placated with a caress, are overcome by a big hug and won over if given a reward, a sweet or an object they like. They love gifts, which they keep

and look after. They also like nature and suffer if kept indoors. As soon as possible, take them out to play on the grass, let them run around in playgrounds. Ideally, they should be encouraged to walk barefoot in parks in order to be in contact with the earth. Having an animal as a companion would make them very happy, and they would certainly take good care of it.

Music Associated

Taurus is famous for its correspondence with singing, and a great many of the leading singers of opera, light and rock music often have Taurus qualities in their birth charts. But, the history of music also boasts extraordinary Taurus composers, from Claudio Monteverdi and Alessandro Scarlatti to Johannes Brahms and Tchaikovsky. Again, in the world of classical music, one of its great violinists, Yehudi Menuhin, was born under Taurus. And Taurus boasts two great singers, Ella Fitzgerald, and Barbra Streisand. Another Taurus celebrity is Charles Mingus, one of the most remarkable jazz musicians and composers, whose pulsating music, so amazingly expressive, transmits all the vigor and energy of the first of the Earth signs, with sudden intervals of extremely moving and lyrical passages. Rock music has a lot of Taurus stars, including Bono, Joe Cocker, Cher, Stevie Wonder, and Mike Old-

with Taurus

field, and Robert Fripp. Another Taurus is the fine late 19th- and early 20th-century classical composer Erik Satie, whose repetitive, bewitching music is based on slow, typically Taurus, melodies that create almost surreal atmospheres in which the listeners' senses are overwhelmed in a meditative dimension that is at once physical and other-worldly. All these Taurus musicians, singers and composers confirm the natural power of the Earth element, in which the triumph of sensuality takes place through rhythmical development that is never aggressive or violent, nor is it ever cold, abstract or too cerebral. Taurus music has an immediate, beneficial effect on one's heart, skin and entire body.

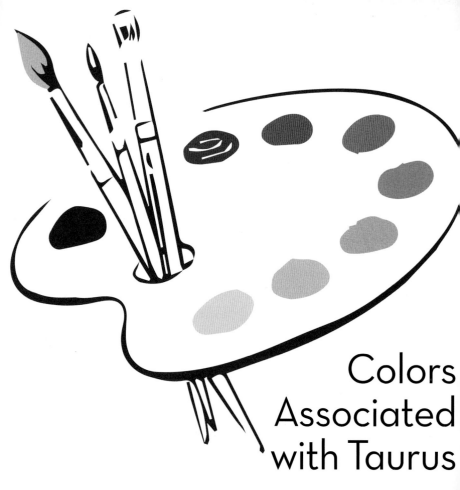

Colors
Associated
with Taurus

The Taurus color is green, which is created by the combination of yellow (jealousy, power, and energy) and blue (spirituality, placidity, discretion). It is a soothing, pure color that is connected to relaxation, the generating harmony of the universe. It is the color of the fertile earth, of luxuriant nature, of the Mother that nourishes us all, the raw material.

In the ancient Egyptian pantheon, the goddess of the sky and birth, Nut, was green. The ancient Greeks called Demeter, the goddess of fertility, 'green ear of wheat'. Green is the color sacred to Venus, the ruling planet of Taurus. It is non-violent and tranquil, like Taurus. Goethe recommended that we put green wallpaper in our apartments and, above all, in the bedroom, because the great German author believed that this color had a calming effect. Green is the color of love, because when love stories begin they are unripe, like green fruit, hence time will make them ripen, and only true love will become a fruit that is no longer sour but ready to enjoy. But, green is also the color of chance, unstable and unpredictable destiny, gambling and fortune. One gambles on a green baize table. For Christians, green is the color of hope, while for Muslims it symbolizes salvation and both material and spiritual wealth. If you want to attract attention, choose a warm, luxuriant color like myrtle green. Veronese green, discovered by the great painter Paolo Veronese, should be used if you want to unleash your creative nature, while emerald green is perfect for feeling well and appearing luminous and brilliant.

Use Celadon green to make a request, ask to be forgiven or get 'yes' for an answer. Jade green is to be worn if you want to express your deepest, most sincere feelings. Sea green is useful is you want to display only the superficial part of yourselves, not the profound one, which others must work at in order to grasp.

Flowers
and Plants
Associated
with
Taurus

Taurus is the sign of nature and needs contact with the earth. Taking care of a garden, a kitchen garden or flowers on a balcony is much better than going to psychiatrist for Taurus. They draw unknown archetypical power from their contact with the earth. Walking on grass is very good for them, especially if it is a meadow of clover or alfalfa. Sacred plants are evergreens such as pine, palm, laurel and box trees. The rose is their flower par excellence, and certain plants ruled by Venus are also very much appreciated: verbena, maidenhair fern and moss.

The following are their personal flowers and plants for each ten-day period.

First period (April 21-30): melissa (lemon balm). This spontaneous, rustic aromatic herb with brightly colored flowers is a favorite with bees. Synonymous with simplicity and gentleness, it sweetens the Taurus temperament. Hold melissa in your hands or drink it as a tisane to change the color of a gloomy day.

Second period (May 1-10): ginger. This plant, of Far Eastern origin, is known mostly by Europeans for its edible rhizome, because it thrives in tropical zones. Should you come near its greenish-yellow flowers, breathe in its scent, since it strengthens your aura. It is equally auspicious if you keep a piece of ginger with you, because in the past people believed that it facilitated any endeavor and helped one to overcome all sorts of difficulty.

Third period (May 11-20): rose. The queen of May and queen of flowers, the rose is connected to love, relations, the emotional and sentimental sphere. For the third ten-day period, it is a precious talisman that increases your fascination and sensuality, gains sympathy and intriguing feeling. Mix its petals with verbena and periwinkle leaves and flowers, then put them in a green sachet and take it with you if you want enjoy an unforgettable romantic rendezvous.

Animals Associated with Taurus

Bulls and bovines in general are the animals that most match your Zodiac sign. The bull evokes the idea of irresistible power and strength, but it is also the symbol of generative and creative strength and represents sexual energy. In Greek mythology, Zeus took on the form of a white bull in order to court and possess Europa. The mount of the Hindu god Shiva is a bull, Nandi, which represents justice, strength and fertility. By riding it, he dominates and transforms sexual energy into spiritual energy. Bull horns, in the shape of a sickle, symbolize the moon, which reminds humanity that this calm and powerful animal is associated with the Great Mother. In fact, in ancient mythology the primeval bull deposited its sperm in the night star. The bull represents your indefatigable spirit, which is capable of unimaginable sacrifices and exertion, and your lunar soul, which is solitary, maternal and poetic.

Other animals in tune with Taurus are rabbits, sheep and goats, which are meek, docile and prolific animals that are very attentive to their offspring and have good relations with humans. Venus is often painted, beautiful and smiling, on a chariot drawn by two white swans. The swan is the symbol of purity and beauty, elegance and nobility. But, it also the symbol of music and song, hence perfect as the embodiment of your natural attractiveness, your love for music and your voice, which is quite often golden. The other birds that astrological tradition attributes to Taurus are the swallow and the pelican.

Among fish associated with Taurus are such freshwater ones as perch, sturgeon, chub and koi carp. The last-mentioned is a Japanese fish with varied and splendid colors that symbolize love, affection and friendship – feelings that you shower, like a warm cloak, on those who are lucky enough to be close to you.

Gemstones Associated with Taurus

All green stones and gems are considered beneficial for Taurus. Among these, first place goes to the emerald, a stone that the ancient Greeks consecrated to Aphrodite. The connection with the goddess of love and beauty means that the emerald facilitates love relationships and relationships in general, and lends quality to your romantic life. Oriental populations believed that the emerald stimulated the memory, strengthened intellectual faculties and protected eyesight. In all ages, this stone has been considered a powerful talisman. A mysterious gem containing secret knowledge, the emerald has a positive and negative side, both a beneficial and malefic aspect. According to Hermeticism, this stone was taken from Lucifer's forehead during his fall from Paradise. In the Middle Ages it was believed that it allowed one to call forth and subjugate evil spirits. According to the 16th-century physician, mathematician and astrologist Gerolamo Cardano, when worn on one's left arm (best if mounted on copper, the metal sacred to Venus), the emerald would protect you from spells and witchery in general. When mounted on a ring and worn on the middle finger it stimulates eloquence. On the other hand, exponents of crystal therapy believe it transmits the spirit of Gaia, Mother Earth, triggering the will to live and favoring self-healing. Placed on the navel it stimulates purification in the kidneys and gall bladder, and when placed on the upper chest it is beneficial for the heart. Whether it guarantees love or healthy energy, the emerald produces synergy with Taurus, transmits your fascinating grittiness and gives you strength to overcome those who provoke you or try to obstruct you. If you want to stir passion and erotic feelings and conquer another, wear opal with an emerald. Jade, less potent but still beneficial for Taurus, should be worn to attenuate certain egoistic and possessive sides of your character, greed, and frustration when you want more of something.

Best Food for Taurus

Taurus is a gourmand and, often, an excellent cook as well, naturally inclined to choose ingredients and combinations very carefully when preparing a meal or eating in a restaurant. They are ruled by Venus, hence an epicurean and a hedonist; they like to live well and savor life, enjoy pleasant sensations and prefer sweet, fragrant, tasty food. As for fruit, they appreciate strawberries, cherries, sour cherries, apricots, medlar and kiwi. But, figs are the fruit most beneficial for and compatible with Taurus. The fig is a Venusian plant, and, with olives and grapes, is one of the fruits that best symbolize abundance, prosperity, and health. The sacred fig tree is the symbol of wisdom, immortality and supreme knowledge in many cultures (Buddha often taught his disciples while seated under a fig tree), fertility and purity in others (Adam and Eve, filled with shame, cover their nudity with fig leaves). And, if we add that figs are rich in potassium, iron, calcium and vitamin B6, it is quite clear that this has to be the favorite fruit of Taurus. But, don't eat too much unless absolutely necessary, because it has laxative properties.

Among the aromatic herbs, Taurus prefers thyme. The name comes from the Greek *thymos* and means strength and courage. It is easy to grow, either in the garden or in the home. If you have an onerous task to see to, a decrease in energy, or are afraid of being abandoned, you can breathe in its scent or season your food with it to benefit from its antiseptic properties on a gastrointestinal level.

While the rose is your flower par excellence, dog rose is your food par excellence. It is a wild plant that forms impenetrable shrubs, like your character at times. Its flowers, leaves and fruit, so rich in vitamin C, are used as a remedy for certain ailments. Use dog rose in tisanes and for making jam.

Myths
Associated
with Taurus

The strong bond Taurus has with the Great Mother Earth, with the generating earth that may be prodigal as well as ungenerous, can be seen in the myth of Demeter. The goddess of harvests, fertility of the land, agriculture, the seasons and the cycle of life and death, Demeter (Ceres for the ancient Romans) had a daughter, Persephone. Hades, the god of the underworld, who was attracted to the young girl when he saw her playing with some nymphs, abducted her, and took her to his underground abode. Demeter became desperate and wandered for days in search of her daughter, in vain. In the meantime, nothing grew in the earth, all the plants withered and died. In order to avoid the extinction of all living things, Zeus forced Hades to free Persephone. As soon as Demeter could embrace her daughter, everything began to bloom again.

Demeter symbolizes the rebirth of nature, just as Taurus symbolizes the dew that penetrates the earth in May. Taurus is synonymous with vital impetus; like the earth, it is patient, persevering and generous. Taurus gives so much, at times too much, to the point of collapsing, but is also prone to taking everything away, making love or a relationship wilt if they feel betrayed or no longer able to trust the other person.

The other goddess connected to Taurus is Hathor, the ancient Egyptian divinity depicted with a woman's face and a cow's horns on her head that frame the disc of the Sun. She is also portrayed as a large cow whose belly represents the firmament, personifying the creator sky, described in ancient texts as "the Great Celestial Cow who created the world and the Sun."

Then, there is the Minotaur, the creature in Greek mythology with a human body and a bull's head who symbolizes the duality, the two extremes, of the Taurus character. At times, Taurus is a placid ox, a cow that grazes peacefully in the meadow. This is the taciturn, detached side, which prefers a quiet life. At other times, Taurus has flaming nostrils and is ready to gore. This expansive, agitated side cannot control its instincts.

Taurus Fairy Tale

The tale of the Three Little Pigs begins when they say goodbye to their mother and set off to build their houses. Of the three, only one was far-sighted and wise. The other two preferred to sing, dance and play rather than be responsible and work hard. They did not want to waste time and energy building their houses, so one made his of straw and the other of sticks. The judicious little pig, on the other hand, built a solid house made of bricks. The Big Bad Wolf had no trouble blowing down the straw and stick houses. The two silly Little Pigs took shelter in their brother's brick house, which the wolf was unable to blow down. The wolf, humiliated and depressed, ran off and the three pigs celebrated happily together.

Like all fairy tales, *The Three Little Pigs* has interesting metaphors, and they correspond to Taurus. The house symbolizes protection, warmth, life, an enclosed circle. Symbolically, it is feminine because it represents shelter, a cozy, intimate atmosphere, the mother's breast. In fact, your house is your world, it is there that you do whatever you want and welcome visits only from those you want. Due to your need for peace and quiet, at times you exaggerate, pushing this behavior to the point of isolating yourselves, passing entire days in splendid solitude. The tale also refers to your industriousness, your great sense of duty, and your indefatigable strength of character. Just like the wise little pig, you are not daunted by hard work. You do not initiate a project unless you know that you can carry it through, and the grit and tenacity you employ to achieve a goal is remarkable. Your strength, which comes to the fore slowly but surely, is capable of great achievements. The story of the Three Little Pigs also symbolizes growth and maturity nourished by awareness. You know how to learn from experience, and examine all factors before making a decision.

PATRIZIA TRONI, trained at the school of Marco Pesatori, writes the astrology columns for Italian magazines *Marie Claire* and *Telepiù*. She has worked in the most important astrology magazines (*Astra, Sirio, Astrella, Minima Astrologica*), she has edited and written the astrology supplement of *TV Sorrisi e Canzoni* and *Chi* for years, and she is an expert not only in contemporary astrology, but also in Arab and Renaissance astrology.

WS White Star Publishers® is a registered trademark property of De Agostini Libri S.p.A.

© 2015 De Agostini Libri S.p.A.
Via G. da Verrazano, 15 - 28100 Novara, Italy
www.whitestar.it - www.deagostini.it

Translation: Richard Pierce - Editing: Norman Gilligan

ISBN 978-88-544-0964-4
1 2 3 4 5 6   19 18 17 16 15

Printed in China